My Profession

Neal Whitman

Cyberwit.net
HIG 45 Kaushambi Kunj, Kalindipuram
Allahabad - 211011 (U.P.) India
http://www.cyberwit.net
Tel: +(91) 9415091004
E-mail: info@cyberwit.net

Printed at Quarterfold Printabilities.

dedicated to Elaine, the love of my life

"Of all the gin joints in all the towns in all the world, she walked into mine."

Humphrey Bogart after spotting Ingrid Bergman seated in his *Rick's Café Americain,* the principal set of the classic movie, *Casablanca.*

Well, it wasn't a gin joint, but a statistics course at Columbia University where learning how to calculate standard deviations would soon lead us to traipsing after our Tuesday night class to the fabled West End Bar for margaritas and cheeseburgers. To riff again on our favorite movie, that was the start of a beautiful friendship that for us bloomed into a loving relationship. A bonus that would blossom years later when I took up the profession of poetry was to be married to a woman who knows when my drafts need to be shaken or stirred.

PREFACE

The word, profession, has its roots in the Latin, *profiteri*, to declare openly. With this collection of my poems, I avow that I believe poetry to be a heart-to-heart connection that is universal. Having a profession also can reference an occupation that requires some higher level of training. Although some poets acquire such, it is not essential. It so happens that my first profession did require graduate level education as a Doctor of Education who worked along side Doctors of Medicine to strengthen the education mission of medical schools … the two other legs of the stool — medical research and clinical service — were outside my training and purview.

One belief I came to hold dearly was that the Arts — literary, performing, and visual — had much to offer, not replace, but supplement the Science of Medicine. In my years as a medical education professional, it should come as no surprise from these prefatory comments, that I introduced medical teachers and students to visiting poets and to poetry, even though at the time I did not write my own poems. In retirement and honored as *professor emeritus* from the University of Utah School of Medicine, how did it come about that I took up a second profession as a poet, not aiming to generate financial gain, but to seek, as a writer, heart-to-heart communication with readers?

It all started at Tor House, the stone cottage Robinson Jeffers built on Carmel Point on California's Monterey Peninsula where I volunteered to be a docent. It was life-changing for me to share his poetry with visitors. When poet Molly Fisk won the 2005 Jeffers Award, I discovered that she conducts an online workshop:

POETRY BOOT CAMP

On a lark, I signed up! For six days, 15 "boot campers" wrote one poem a day. We critiqued each others poems … and Molly even critiqued our critiques! When the workshop was over, it was not "over" for me. My wife that summer was undergoing chemotherapy for breast cancer. Pencil in hand, notebook in lap, I wrote poems waiting with her in the infusion center. What did I write? You might be surprised, but I wrote about anything and everything *not* about cancer. That was my "spousal therapy."When the treatments were over, I realized that I had more poems in me. I was ready to write about light and dark and shadows and the shadows cast on us. Thereafter I made it my profession to read or write poetry every day. Now I avow a second and life-long profession. I write to be read, so it has exceeded my expectations that north of 1000 general poems and also the same of Japanese form haiku and tanka have been published.

I was thrilled when Managing Editor Dr. Karunesh Kumar Agarwal asked to publish a book of my haiku (*From This Moment On*) and tanka (*How Pleasant It Is*) in 2020 and now to ask to bring out a book of my general poems. As you will see, the poems in this collection have been culled from the awards podium … not room for all "winners" but these are my favorites. I offer awarded poems not to boast, but to depend on esteemed poets who judge contests that these are "worthies".

I sign off with two beliefs I profess: no two people read the same poem and no one reads the same poem twice. So, I hope there are poems here that will please some of you now, and, if not now, will some day in the future.

Contents

Listening to Cheese 9

Opening the Window 10

Context is All 12

Simple to Harvest, Hard to Find 13

The Secret of the Esselen 14

At Whit's End 15

Der Taschenspieler 16

I Wish I Might 18

What We Found Under the Waterfall: Thomas Hardy cento 19

Seven Ways to Prepare for Lengthening Days 20

4 Songs of Tzu-Yeh 22

Two Paths Cross 24

Four Old Men 26

My Mentor's Last Poem 27

Ancient Music 28

All the Way Down 29

She Was a Paul Girl 30

Villanelle Vows 31

Sunday Night in His Kennel 32

Out, Not In 33

Still, Still 34

For the Time Being: Double Shijo 36

When Dusk Falls 37

A Chess Game, I Guess 38

Music to My Ears 39

What if you had eyes 40

on the inside of your mouth? 40

King Duncan's Porter Invents the Knock, Knock Joke
and Kills the Audience 41

kerplunk 43

Paying Tribute 45

Assignation: Cherita* in Five Parts 46

Dobro jutro [Good morning] 48

Breathe Deeply 50

Limpets Make Good Teachers 51

He Taught Us Not to Fear the Abyss 52

Moving out, Moving on 53

Oh, Mistress Dickinson, why not peonies? 54

Prompted by Pliny the Elder* 55

Gremorse 56

Way to Go 57

Second Marriage: Renewal of Faith in Love 58

I Have Good News 59

Psalm 150.1 60

I'll Take a Z, Vanna 61

The Thing Is: It Takes as Long as It Takes 62

The Sea Around Us 63

How to Charm a Critic 64

The Gift They Leave Us 65

Bixby Bridge 66

A Trial before the 42 Judges of Osiris* 67

A Lover's Lament: ryuka quintet 68

Ho Attraversata Tutta la Città 69

inspired by Antonio Vivaldi, Le Quattro Stagioni. 70

Typo-logy 72

When Days Get Short 73

Who ... oops ... Whom Do You Trust? 74

Poets are the Canis lupus familiaris 75

of Homo sapiens 75

Lofty Aspirations 76

Listening to Cheese

G.K. Chesterton was known for his mystery stories.
"Poets," he once declaimed," "have been mysteriously silent
on the subject of cheese."
I make a long distance call:

"Oh, Higher Authority." [some call this God, others their Muse],
"Let me listen to cheese."

Cut to the scene:
A wine and cheese reception at a Bloor-Yorkville art gallery.
Gallo by the gallon in plastic cups.
Cubed cheese, yellow and white.

"Pat, come here. Look at this still life.
The one with the chunk of cheese on a plate.
Wouldn't it look great over the table
we got in that consignment shop?"

"Susan, ya gotta be kiddin'. It's so... It's so... it's so...
SUPERFLUOUS."

Susan and Pat replenish their plates.
I remain.
I listen to the cheese.
I hear a cold, damp cave.
I hear a French ballad... no, not French, Norman... no, not a ballad, a
villanelle.
It tells me, "An Ontario Icewine will do nicely!"
And I buy it.

2009 James McIntyre Poetry Contest 1st place

Opening the Window

I begin
in the lower left corner,
testing the solution that will
remove dirt and grime. In the lingo of my trade
we call this "opening the window."
Rembrandt
sits on my easel awaiting restoration:
Portrait of the Painter in Old Age.

I choose from
a dozen small jars,
compounds concocted by trial and error.
Only teachable things can be taught, but
flair is not among these.
If not for the out-take vent
linseed and acetate odors would fill the studio.
Aromatics can smell pleasant,

but are toxic.
With lumps of white bread
I remove dust and soot stuck on the surface
and gently wipe with a swab. Donning
magnified goggles,
I gently poke with a sharpened chopstick, adding
dabs of color.
My final touch: anti-fungal spray.

Bringing back a painting
is part chemistry,
part art, part instinct.
Only a callous,
sensitive thumb can lift yellowed varnish
and leave the paint intact. Untrained
fingers can damage.
A fine scalpel is of little use in the wrong hands.

Blistering, blanching, browning:
the effects of aging
spare no one.
When my work is done,
two old men
appraise each other. We like what we see.
As I look in, he looks out
through the opened window.

2010 Common Ground Review Contest 3rd place

Context is All

"Hell is someplace where nothing connects to nothing."
   T.S Eliot commenting on Dante's *Inferno*

That evening
the children were given no homework.
The mimeo machine is broken, again?
Start of school vacation?
A reward for good work?
So many good reasons.
But what if…
on February 17, 1944,
Jews were leaving their Italian captors in the morning?
Taken by the German Waffen-SS:
650 men, women, and children
packed and stacked in train wagons.
And sent off into morning fog?
From Turin, North then East.
East past Austrian towns.
East past Czech towns, Slovakian towns.
East to Auschwitz.
Journey to nothingness. In the Italian camp,
the little school run by the women inmates had continued
to the last day. But that evening
the children were given no homework.
All took leave that night.
All took leave from Life.
All were taken someplace where nothing connects to nothing.
All were taken to the Inferno.

2010 Common Ground Review Contest honorable mention

Simple to Harvest, Hard to Find

in the fall season after a rainy spell
 he wakes early and heads outdoors
  to his secret spots
   his cache prize
    under moss
     pay
      dirt

     artist and naturalist
     a wild mushroom forager
     Marty has been harvesting
     edibles for thirty years

      the
      pine
     mushroom:
      matsutake
    highly prized and rare
   spicy-aromatic odor
concealed under leaves and duff on forest floor

2011 Common Ground Review Contest finalist

The Secret of the Esselen

When you sit long enough
the low-lying scrub
begin to sway
not with the wind
but of their own volition.
It takes time
for them to trust you.

When you sit long enough
the tree top branches
welcome waves of fog
and gently push
the mist inland.
It takes time
for the cloud-tide to rise.

When you sit long enough
you become aware you are
under cloud, in cloud, breathing cloud
and licking your lips
taste sea salt.
It takes time
to keep a secret.

2011 Angels without Wings Chief's Choice Award

At Whit's End

Poetry is the source
for my humble gifting.
Hearty without remorse
must be spirit lifting.

I spare no words
to rhyme or reason.
But words too obtuse
are a poet's treason.

My poem is done–
it's ready for bed.
Its title a pun–
I hope it's been read.

My work is completed
and closed like the day;
The Hand that wrote it
now lays it away.

2011 The Oak, K. Blaze Memorial Prize Winner

Der Taschenspieler

i. allegro

Itzhak Perlman comes on stage.
Takes one step at a time slowly.
Reaches his chair and sits down.
Puts his crutches on the floor and unclasps his leg braces.
Picks up his violin, puts it under his chin, nods to the conductor.
And off we go. Mozart's 4th Concerto: festive, bright, beguiling.
But then we hear it. A sound like a gun shot.
One of the strings has snapped.

ii. andante

I saw this happen once before.
Pinchas Zukerman was in town.
He exchanged violins with the concertmaster without missing a
beat.
Tonight the orchestra stops.
Perlman takes a breath.
Signals the conductor to begin again.
I can see him re-composing the piece in his head.
Re-tunes strings to get the sounds he wants.

iii. rondeau

An old, yet new piece of music.
Variation on a Mozart Concerto in Three Strings.
Its finale. We are dancing.
We are done. On our feet.

The Magician smiles. Wipes the sweat from his brow.
Raises his bow to quiet us and announces:
"You know, sometimes it is the artist's task to find out
how much music you can still make with what you have left."

2011 Angels without Wings Foundation Honor Scroll Award

I Wish I Might

i. miss you in the morning
the smell of old sheets
your empty pillow next to mine
listening to the ticking
it's been a year now
her sweater still on the chair

ii. miss you on the dunes
we were for the birds
today I found a pelican feather
now a bloodless shaft
I bring back words like stones
still wet when the tide recedes

iii.
miss you in the stars
alone on a moonless night
I am for the dark.
wished upon a star
with you on a night like this
when we were for the dark

2011 Lincoln Library at Twelve Bridges Contest 3rd place

What We Found Under the Waterfall:
Thomas Hardy cento

by the runlet's rim
where we sat to dine
   we spied an ouzel
   swimming under water
   it leapt out of the brook
   and landed on flat rock
   in its beak a squirming prize

in the burn of August
to paint the scene
   sun had followed rain
   and we found a spot
   where we might be alone
   wild foxglove and fern
   lined our dining floor

we placed our basket
of fruit and wine
   the dipper took flight
   and taking its morsel
   flew though the waterfall
   perhaps a fool-hardy thing to do
   we waded into the arched cave

under a sky of blue
with a leaf-wove awning
   there behind the falls
   a nest of soft green moss —
   two baby water birds
   learning a water song
   peee peee pijur pijur

2012 Common Ground Review Contest Finalist

Seven Ways to Prepare for Lengthening Days

Wash your hair with lavender water
and air-dry outside your front door.
This is the way
we come clean.

Sweep your home
and fill the space with kindness.
This is the way
we make space.

Burn pine needles in bundles
and gently blow out the flame.
This is the way
we clear the air.

Collect porcupine quills
and blue jay feathers.
This is the way
we find words.

Make signals in shallow water
and wave to stones.
This is the way
we welcome guests.

Sit under the early evening sky
and wait for the first star.
This is the way
we enter the universe.

Hold the moon in your chest
and have a pure heart.
This is the way
we love.

2012 Angels without Wings Poet Laureate

4 Songs of Tzu-Yeh

Tzu-Yeh is the name of a legendary wineshop girl in 4th century China who wrote song-poems. Whether or not there was such a person, this is a form of poetry named for her. It is rendered in four couplets and the challenge for the contemporary poet, who might be female or male, young or old, Oriental or Occidental, is to convey a down-to-earth, folk-like "shop girl" experience.

1. Shining

Awake? if awake, joy
    in the waking hour
in the wee waking hour
    stretch stretch
iron pot and bamboo whisk
    morning tea
hyacinths and biscuits
    breakfast fare

2. Walking

the ash slat boardwalk
    welcomes me
nodding to passersby
    we know our way
unlock the iron gate
    the shop is mine alone
soon customers arrive
    my crescent smile

3. Ending

a moon sliver
    at the edge of twilight
appears against the tender blue
    of early night.
how weak is the light
    and my promise not to miss him
if I had been capable of a song
    I would have sung it

4. Longing

the orchid I brought home
    from the street stall last week
has turned a dismal hue
    standing alone
night is a monotonous period
    when only one cricket crickets
and not one cares for me
    tonight tonight

2012 Dancing Poetry Festival 3rd prize

Two Paths Cross

The sanctuary at dawn
poet and photographer
each one there to shape worth
grass bending under gentle wind
the Earth axis tilting toward the sun
here and now, no where else to be

syllable count does not make a poem
#2 pencil does not write a poem
equipment does not take a photograph
a camera is of little use to the untrained eye
not the form, but the vision is essential
here and now, the ah-ness of early summer

just one thing happens at a time
one thing captures your attention
and you show it
the flash of ultimate reality
in word or image
honeybee and hummingbird

one rule of poem:
two images that do
and do not go together
a rule of composition:
two subjects that cause the viewer
to look back and forth

the poem not read is unfinished
the photograph not seen is undeveloped
the poet points at shadows
the photographer exposes light
honey bee and hummingbird
drink the holy nectar

2013 The Oak, K. Blaze Memorial Prize Winner

Four Old Men

Le tseat
French noun, masculine
émigré from Czarist Russia
"The battle has not ceased,
but has taken on new forms."

Let seat
Imperative
Gent on public transit rises.
"I see you are in a family way.
Sit."

Let's eat
Injunction
Thanksgiving Day
"The turkey is done. Turn off the TV.
The Lions are down by how much?"

Letse at
Name of Sung Dynasty poet
He had two pupils
in his right eye.
"I lift the curtain and see purple cliffs."

 2013 Angels without Wings Foundation Honor Scroll
Award,

My Mentor's Last Poem

green tea steeping in a thrift shop teapot
bittersweet, buttery aroma
on a plate an apple sliced thin
one sees most by candlelight
when one sees so little
I saved his letter
to be the last
this evening
now pour
sip

as
his mind
was slipping
his pen refused
to spell correctly
and he apologized
for his wretched handwriting
and for the length of his poem
explaining that he did not have time
to commit his verse to fewer pages

2013 Thief River Falls Library 2nd prize

Ancient Music

From the wing bone of a mute swan
music filled a cave 35,000 years ago —
a 3-hole flute fashioned to express
joy and sorrow. Music at the end
still the natural way to go. Yes, the heart
must beat to live. Yes, brain waves
signal life spark. Still, we note the end
by our last breath. Her 6-hole wood flute
custom made for Hospice, long for low notes,
thin so light to hold. She follows the breath
of the patient. Starts and stops with him.
The sound of the flute following, not leading.
He takes his last breath.
Now soundless.

2014 Bay Area Poets Coalition honorable mention

All the Way Down

A professor from the local college
speaks to the Senior Center.
He gives a scientifically sound talk
on how the universe was made.
One woman in the back row waves her hand.
"Sonny," she said, "you got it all wrong."
She explains that the world sits on …
a giant turtle!
The scientist asks, with a smug smile,
what the turtle sits on? She triumphs:
"An endless pile of turtles, one on top of another."
Yes, of course.

2014 California Federation of Chaparral Poets 2nd place

She Was a Paul Girl

On my belly, I am propped on elbows
with my head cradled in my hands.
It was a Sunday night ritual:
my family watches The Ed Sullivan Show.

Forty years later her head
is cradled in my hands.
My mother has broken her hip,
and now pneumonia has set in.

She opened her eyes and said,
"I'm a Paul Girl."
She closed her eyes
and slept the morphine sleep.

 I sang (well, whispered)
"In my hour of darkness
she is speaking words of wisdom.
Let it be, let it be."

2014 The Oak, Minnie Memorial Winner

Villanelle Vows

All that is in this delightful garden grows,
Should happy be, and have immortal bliss.
Edmund Spenser, Faerie Queene, st. 41

Have immortal bliss.
Bride and Groom: "Dost thou?"
And now you may kiss.

We to bear witness
two to make a vow.
Have immortal bliss.

Nothing here amiss
if each day lived now.
And now you may kiss.

One of you remiss?
Forgive and allow.
Have immortal bliss

Then in all fairness
to bend like a bough.
And now you may kiss.

Leave today with this:
Every day endow.
Have immortal bliss.
And now you may kiss.

2014 New England Poetry Club Boyle-Faber Memorial honorable mention

Sunday Night in His Kennel

Out of sound – All night in the unmade park
Shut in shut out thorncrazed tinglefinger
Death fathers all – The sombre bell at dark

Unpockets papers found – cache for this clerk
Dead as a dodo boyblazed beehounder
Out of sound – All night in the unmade park

Tender for his journal – needs but a spark
Shut down shut up a fistcupped heartdragger
Death fathers all – The sombre bell at dark

His pencil dull – it needs to be made sharp
Dead as a door knob root-tapped mulchdigger
Out of sound – All night in the unmade park

"Time is, time is done" – a quotation mark
Soliciting crookboned strifeplanter
Death fathers all – The sombre bell at dark

Don't let the lies rip in half your bookmark
Truth is a shear bolt tooledged mindchanger
Out of sound – All night in the unmade park
Death fathers all – The sombre bell at dark

2014 The Colour of Saying:
A Creative Writing Competition in Celebration of Dylan
Thomas

Out, Not In

after a Persian tale

A woman long living alone
bought a parrot to keep her company.
She tried to teach it to talk,
but her house remained empty of conversation.
So, she put out a "room for rent" sign
and a student of philosophy moved in.
He left early his first day and returned late.
The woman asked where he was when he was out.
He answered that when he was out, he was not in.
Remember: I told you he was a student of philosophy.
The next day the student again
left early and returned late,
this time bringing home a crow hit in traffic.
With the crow now sharing his cage,
the parrot spoke its very first words,
"Where did they find such a hideous creature?"
The crow thought,
"What misfortune to be paired with this babbling idiot."

2014 Amici di Guido Gozzano Attesto di Merito

Still, Still

We must be still and still moving
Into another intensity
For a further union…
     T.S. Eliot, East Coker, *Four Quartets*
There is still movement.
Well, maybe not still, but unseen,
like that green moth flexing wings
that suddenly lifts with it the brown field.
All sleep under this blanket of dusk.
We are one kind. No one is unkind.

The townswoman in *High Noon* asks,
"What's the matter with you people?"
It is ten minutes to noon. It is not too late.
There is still time– time that does not move.
The DVD I rented is skipping so I fast forward,
but it freezes before Amy leaves on the noon train.

A poet invites me to *Poetski Maraton* in Sarajevo.
His one American is sick and cancelled. It is in six days.
Sabi says he is sorry to ask me "at ten minutes to noon."
This Bosnian tells me we need to lose someone
to know kindness. He butters me up a little.
How would he say that in his language?

Sabi adds that he likes the part in my poem
he translated where the uncle in the garden
tells his nephew that he, the uncle,
needs to be circumcised. Didn't I write

that, like a garden, he needed to be "pruned"?
As least that is what I understood him to say.

My Serbo-Croatian is rusty… well, in truth, non-existent.
And, my Italian? It's English with vowels at the end of words.
Montale, speaking to his dead wife, told her that she alone knew
that movement and stasis were one. But both knew.
And we do too: *We are a single thing-a. Capiche?*
Still, with regret, I tell Sabi I cannot go. I needed more time.

*2015 United Poets Laureate International Founders
Memorial Finalist*

For the Time Being: Double Shijo

i. I like to walk along the shore at the crack of dawn
and taste sea salt on my dry lips.
When the wind cuts across cresting waves
water particles rise to form a natural prism.
This magical aerial play to start the day
disappears before the next wave arrives.

ii. Mist settles on the bay and I see nothing but mist,
so I depend upon seal barks to know where I am.
Below me must be the pinniped haul-out
where yesterday I lost my woolen scarf.
It is unraveling, but is still my favorite,
Hand-knit by her so very long ago.

The author was inspired by the Sung-Il Lee's translation of 3-line
Korean form of Shijo into 6-line English.

2015 United Poets Laureate International finalist

When Dusk Falls

response to *Wandering Minstrels*, Hubert Robert (1779)

In a panel from the Bagatelle series
we find ourselves on the *Piazza del Campidoglio.*
Buskers as common as stray cats play for tips.
The painter has returned to his *appartamento.*

Three minstrels sit on the steps
to split the proceeds equally –
reckoning at the end of day.
The old guitarist is known to cheat.

After the sun sets they find a bench
to share *la carne dei poveri* and rough *vino rossi* –
reckoning at the end of day.
The old guitarist is known to cheat.

2015 Amici di Guido Gozzano Attesto di Merito

A Chess Game, I Guess

Blackie
   was chasing
      Snowball
         down
            the
               stairs.

They saw me and froze.
      Each paused
      with paw
         in
         mid-air
      eyes turned
      toward me.

The black dog
could have pounced
upon its frozen prey
or the white cat
could have fled
from its halted predator.

But it was only
         a game
                  not a hunt
                     that resumed
as soon as I passed on by.

2015 Lincoln Library at Twelve Bridges Contest 2rd place

Music to My Ears

"And death is a low mist which cannot blot the brightness…"
      - Shelley, *Adonais: An Elegy on the Death of John Keats*

Keats
Would take
A hot bath
Dress in his best
Cut a chunk of cheese
Peel and slice an apple
Pour a glass of good red wine
Place cheese, apple, wine at his side
Ask, "Where's the poet? Show him! Show him…"
Dip his quill pen in an ink pot and write
Winchester, rosy-hued late afternoon
No poem perfect – perhaps this one
Sublime in the season of mist
Cheese and apple, sip of wine
Timeless evocation
In thirty-three lines
ode To Autumn
Apple core
Cheese rind
Blot

2013 Dancing Poetry International 3rd place

What if you had eyes

on the inside of your mouth?

Would no longer fear
half-worm in the apple

Nor fret a fish bone
stuck in your craw

Chewing the fat
supersedes psychobabble

No unsightly tooth-smile
dratted carrot in coleslaw

2016 Bay Area Poets Coalition 1st prize

King Duncan's Porter Invents the Knock, Knock Joke and Kills the Audience

in remembrance of 400th anniversary of Shakespeare's death

Knock, Knock.
Who's there?
Ferris.
Ferris who?
Ferris foul, and foul is fair,
Hover through the fog and filthy air.
Shut in. Shut out.
Shut up. Shut down.
Dead as Duncan.
Dead as a door nail.
Make the door. Make it fast.
No trespassing. No soliciting.
Don't let the lies out.
Truth is a deadbolt.
I live in a place no one knows.

Knock, Knock.
Who's there?
Leon.
Leon who?
Leon MacDuff
And damned be him that first cries
"Hold, enough!"
In this house perfect silence.
You want to catch a mouse?

You got to think like a mouse.
At midnight
scratchings in the wall.
In the morning I check the trap.
No mouse.
No cheese.

2016 United Poets Laureate International honorable mention

kerplunk

no friend to share / news of my teacher's death /spring rain
Mitsu Suzuki

Mitsu Suzuki
helped her second husband, Shunryu Suzuki,
establish the San Francisco Zen Center.
Masaharu Matsuno, her first husband,
was a Japanese pilot in World War II.
His job was to choose targets for bombing raids over China.
She wrote to him:

Remember that those are mothers and fathers with children.
Please target rice fields instead of the towns and cities.
Drop bombs to surprise the snails in the rice fields.

Two weeks after she sent Masaharu
a photograph of their newborn daughter,
she learned she was a widow.
Senbei brushed with mirin
was left at her door. Donor unknown.
When others were having a hard time
she would invite them for tea in her kitchen.

January 9, 2016, she leaves us at age 101.
With the news of her passing in Japan,
warm waters cross the Pacific known to us as El Nino.
Rains at last come to Castroville.

Finally fields are wet. I smell garlic and artichoke.
That evening the sun drops in the blink of an eye.
She taught us to count haiku sounds, not syllables

dropping sun / in the blink of an eye / kerplunk
one of her devoted students

2016 United Poets Laureate International honorable mention

Paying Tribute

The poet Shen Yo had two pupils
in his left eye. He was revolting
when the emperor killed his brother.
Time is … time is done.
The human clock struck again.
Death fathers all.

The poet Shen Yo had two pupils.
The three went on a pilgrimage.
and stopped under a grove where
in the hollow, amid ferns,
each left behind
their swords

2016 Common Ground Review Contest 2nd prize

Assignation: Cherita* in Five Parts

i. still morning, still pond

flat stones
skip the surface

I cast my net
north
of the future

ii. future is not my forté

still has two els
each is upright

still I am resolved
to remain constant
without conditions I listen

iii. listen for its whistle

yes, dear …
I will come to you by train

no turbulence
time to gaze, reflect
and, yes, to write love poems

iv. poems blue-penciled into oblivion

my overnight bag
stuffed with many refusals

my editor's rebukes
it's me is now the norm
but still it is she

v. she tells me *hush*

her fingers
cover my mouth

footsteps
on the staircase
*who will make the first move ... keep **still***

* Cherita (pronounced CHAIR-rita), Malay for story or tale, consists of a one-line stanza, followed by a two-line stanza, and then finishing with a three-line stanza

2016 Amici di Guido Gozzano Attesto di Merito

Dobro jutro [Good morning]

I love email because I can have a friend
who lives in Croatia and is a poet.
We call each other "poet-cousins once removed."
When I wake in the morning, from this distant land
Djurdja's greeting is waiting for me: *Dobro jutro.*
Was it sent yesterday, today,
or tomorrow?

She and her husband, Stjepan,
live in a farmhouse built by her grandfather
who came home from The Great War
married to a Russian widow. Not enough
young men returned home -– too few husbands
for too many maidens. Imagine
the gossip.

Djurdja has a cat she found in the woods
abandoned by its mother. She named it Perdita.
This cat follows Djurdja into town like a dog.
Both poets and cats know how to listen.
Djurdja brings home stories from street corners
and shops, which she says "dab" her poems
with local color.

Djurdja tells me that Perdita understands her
by the "color of my voice" and knows when
to lie by her slipper or to hide. Plus, this cat
never steals food: "Good manners are good manners."

At the "crevice of dawn" they "work" the countryside,
collecting quills and small animal bones.
Also, words.

2016 Ina Coolbrith Circle 1st honorable mention

Breathe Deeply

the low sandy beach and the thin scrub pine
Sun has dropped; I prefer the day less bright.
the wide reach of bay and the long skyline

taste of salt on my tongue and smell of brine
Shades of grey; poets see best in twilight.
the low sandy beach and the thin scrub pine

orange and yellow linger, then blush wine
The air cools; colors splay across my sight.
the wide reach of bay and the long skyline

Hindi call it cow dust time -this divine
Silhouettes prevail along the coast's bight.
the low sandy beach and the thin scrub pine

one crow on a bough as if by design
L'heure bleue turns to *noir*; day now truly night.
the wide reach of bay and the long skyline

Pluck two pearls, one pitch black, one purest white.
Polish them with chamois dipped in moonlight.
the low sandy beach and the thin scrub pine
the wide reach of bay and the long skyline

*2016 United Poets Laureate International honorable
mention*

Limpets Make Good Teachers

when the tide turns, not to be caught
in swirling water is no trifle
that is why on rocks limpets squat
each in its own made-to-fit spot
an imperative of survival

on the rising tide off they go
limpets do not travel very far
foraging for food to and fro
scraping algae off rocks below
licking with their fine-toothed radula

how to survive, how to adapt
eight thousand wave crashes a day
out of our depth we can be trapped
Go with the flow. Love is the way.

2016 United Poets Laureate International honorable mention

He Taught Us Not to Fear the Abyss

I hold a glass of soju in two hands and bow slightly –
   though I am alone, I sense his presence.
Seonsaeng-nim* left us one year ago tonight
   but still speaks to us through his poetry.
By his example we learned to stay true to who we are –
   it is the practice of my craft that is the point.

His last letter was smuggled to us –
   a prison guard risked his own freedom.
From inside his cell my old teacher wrote
   that he was a free man in his own right.
Dictators fear poets, but poets feel no fear –
   even when the world is cracked.

At the crevice of dawn I walk along the cliff –
   below me surf crashes against volcanic boulders.
When the wind cuts across cresting waves
   water particles rise to form a natural prism.
This magical aerial display to start the day
   disappears before the next wave arrives.

*In Korean, the word for teacher is *seonsaeng* and then *nim* at
the ending is added to express high regard or esteem for some-
one you are speaking about.

2016 United Poets Laureate International 2nd prize

Moving out, Moving on

No one was home,
I was grateful for the packed bag
and map left on the porch.
I took leave without a word –
next day reported to duty.

Two words –
Fear and Courage
These are the two ends
of one linked chain.
It is no light matter.

I wrote letters.
But, what did I want to say?
A rough sort of content –
I did not have it in me
to attempt cheerful dispatches.

Back in the real world
I struggled to get up and do on –
to live with circumstances.
That is the least I can do.
And, the most.

A turkey vulture ascends –
the current bears him away
Odysseus had it right.
It takes ten years
to return home from war.

2016 Bay Area Poets Coalition 3rd prize

Oh, Mistress Dickinson, why not peonies?

[Emily Dickinson in italics]

living simply
memories
washed by sun showers faith
at the start
pretty rain from those sweet eaves

opened by the wind
windflowers
buried and recovered longing
to please
pray gather me, anemone

the ground flooded
peonies
bent and broken
in her garden
but not found in her verse

in her poems
flowers
abound, bud, bloom, and burst
but not this one … perhaps,
not with a club, the Heart is broken

2017 Amici di Guido Gozzano Attesto di Merito

Prompted by Pliny the Elder*

Nulla dies sine linea. Not a day without a line.

not a day without a line
black on white my pen pours out
fill the vessel up: port wine

scritch for scratch will make it mine
clear the mind, a mapless route
not a day without a line

not a blot, a goodly sign
mop the deck and brush off doubt
fill the vessel up: port wine

dit or dot, rope versus twine
whipping wind, let's turn about
not a day without a line

sounding words hard to define
from crow's nest, a gladly shout
fill the vessel up: port wine

verse, my pen is dipped in brine
sent to editor: sea-scout
not a day without a line
fill the vessel up: port wine

*   Roman naval commander and aphorist who died 79 C.E. of toxic fumes attempting to rescue by ship friends from the eruption of Mt. Vesuvius

2017 Bay Area Poets Coalition 3rd prize

Gremorse

with *grief* and sorrow she did sit to spin
when her Love passed by and did not come in

they lay once in a meadow sweet to rest
while there a woodlark guarded her grass nest

oh, now *remorse* is at her true heart's core
for those dear pleasured days will come no more

in her wee garden one red rose unfolds
with bachelor buttons and with marigolds

her wish to bring him back a little while
the song, the dance, the dawn, the sigh, the smile

a heavy cloud on her brow she does feel
her tangled thoughts turn with the spinning wheel

2018 United Poets Laureate International 3rd prize

Way to Go

laid out
in my Armani suit
cherry casket gleams –
my Friday Men's Club files by
Damn, he looks good ... Aways did!

a simple pine box
like the one that held my chess set –
only been one day
and already am at home ...
the mourner's prayer: *Kaddish**

a coffin
made by Trappist monks
and blessed by them –
old growth wood and no veneer
shaped in rural solitude

I am reduced
to cinder and bone fragments:
basic elements
my ashes float on kelp
all the way to Japan

a pilot program
I am flown to Washington
to be composted –
which may help save our planet
I will rest in peat

*   Jewish prayer recited for the dead

2018 United Poets Laureate International honorable mention

Second Marriage: Renewal of Faith in Love

for Bob and Bobby, August 7, 2017

there can be no doubt
for poor souls two plants
come recommended
the laurel-leaved rock rose
greets the south-west wind
with a lavish out-pouring of fragrance …
here and there as it grows old
a branch breaks
but its old age is neither untidy
nor unsightly, but dignified

the gum rock rose, more tender
may be even more beautiful …
do we regret that its flowers
are so short-lived?
many expand in the morning
to fall at noon
at dusk only by a white pool
of fallen petals on the ground
may we know how fair and full
was the flower at forenoon

2018 Amici di Guido Gozzano Attesto di Merito

I Have Good News

in her blue and white tiled kitchen
she crushes garlic and ginger
chops green beans to be steamed

in boiling water
chickpeas are transformed
without suffering

in the heat of separation
of spirit from body
is there a need to suffer?

eggs separated in a yellow ware bowl –
the one we bartered for
in that estate sale

my wife's cancer journey
this soufflé will not fall

2018 Bay Area Poets Coalition honorable mention

Psalm 150.1

for Leonard Cohen

You grew sick of us and stepped off the planet.
    Too many times we had sung Hallelujah.

For seven days we sat there
    as tears perfused the silted eddies.

Days and more days passed
    and this is what we told ourselves:

All you seem is and now that is done.
    And the river rose and it flowed once more.

And so we were rescued
    and there were little miracles too.

Such as someday our becoming
    roots, trunks, and limbs.

And, for two crows then to perch
    on our branch at dusk.

More than a year has passed
    the time for mourning is over.

Now we realize
    we had been too ready to condemn David.

And would that matter?
    And did you know?

2019 Amici di Guido Gozzano Attesto di Merito

I'll Take a Z, Vanna

you may recall
the origin of the game show
Wheel of Fortune
was Hangman...
so it did seem karmic
when my 88-year old neighbor,
we are told, turned away
the priest at her front door:
"Not a convenient time, Father."
even behind her closed door
he could hear the TV …
as it turned out, that night
was her last spin

2019 Ina Coolbrith Circle 3rd place

The Thing Is: It Takes as Long as It Takes

in his first grieving
he pivots to poetry
to tell his pain

in his second grieving
he wears black in the daytime
to tell the Sun, "No"

in his third grieving
he wears white at nighttime
to tell the Moon, "Me, too"

in his fourth grieving
he steps outside naked
to tell the rain, "Both of us"

in his fifth grieving
he turns the radio knob
to cut out the static

in his sixth grieving
he asks for a kiss
to lure her back

in his seventh grieving
he finally tells it
to give it a rest

2020 California Federation of Chaparral Poets 1st place

The Sea Around Us

between tides
under the sea wind
the edge of the ocean

sand becomes pale
sea turns lavender
twilight

from the bay
far away sounds of evening
beach smells, too

in the sweep
of the lighthouse
a flight of terns

gulls
following a fishing boat
a good catch

2020 California Federation of Chaparral Poets 3rd place

How to Charm a Critic

in a bamboo box
mix thistledown
with wren's nest fluff
leave under new moon
until next day noon
then store it under your bed
here is what an old crone said
when a critic's words wound
here is your charm
to protect you from harm
on the smallest envelope in your home
write the offender's name
warm thumb and forefinger
over a candle flame
from the box, into the envelope,
add two pinches
put this missive in your sock drawer
and what once hurt will no more

*2020 California Federation of Chaparral Poets
honorable mention*

The Gift They Leave Us

with a Fibonacci sequence

we
see
aloft
two lovebirds
after the wedding
nuzzling in an evergreen tree
with the breeze they take to the sky
circle and depart
one feather
spirals
to
Earth

2020 Amici di Guido Gozzano Attesto di Merito

Bixby Bridge

Night comes the hour is rung
The days go I remain
 The Mirabeau Bridge by Guillaume Apollinaire

Bixby Bridge posted
Slippery When Wet
my eyes on the road
not the ocean below
unseen but there

a coastal drive
slowed by pelting rain
my grip tightens
and I stick to the right
because I hate to change lanes

Night, the hour again.
Night comes, the clock sounds.
Strike the hour.
The day departs – I remain
Days pass by – I go, too.

2021 California Federation of Chaparral Poets 2nd prize

A Trial before the 42 Judges of Osiris*

fragment in italics by ancient Egyptian unknown

you … saying …guilty
… they judge my Soul …
… for I have not obeyed …
for I have gone astray
… judge me those who hold the balance…

the text
torn and incomplete
these opening lines
in hieratic papyrus
its origin uncertain

my heart on one plate
on the other, feather of truth –
Osiris,
in the Hall of Judgement,
remember: even trees fall!

*   It was believed in Ancient Egypt that 42 judges in the presence of Osiris, God of the Afterlife, decided if on balance the deceased deserved passage to eternal life.

2021 Amici di Guido Gozzano Menzio d'Onore

A Lover's Lament: ryuka quintet

i. at the Bottom
    her heart is heavy with the weight
    of broken trust and betrayal
    the windlass with each crank and turn
    drops the anchor lower

ii. in the Depths
    across the rippling lake at dusk
    a gentle breeze bends sweet-grass reeds
    as a bamboo flute now pulsates
    in rhythm with her heart

iii. on Balance
    in shallow water, two cranes stand
    each on one leg, neck under wing
    within my breast the thought of you
    sharing a soft pillow

iv for Dismal Hours
    in time out-worn, her heart worn-out
    against the blue-grey of twilight
    light is weak; weak is her promise
    not to miss him by dawn

v. under an Echo
    with a start suddenly I wake
    my heart beating fast with rapture
    you call my name and I cry out
    but there is no reply

2022 California Federation of Chaparral Poets 2nd prize

Ho Attraversata Tutta la Città

[first line of "Trieste" by Umberto Saba]

My long-distance friend, Cara Lidia,
tells me that Italians use the phrase,
un viaggiatore in poltrona for what I am,
which in English we call "an armchair traveler."

My wife prepares a favorite dinner,
scampi alla busara. Ah, now you've guessed!
Settled in my armchair, after dinner
my imaginary destination: Trieste!

Who better to guide me? Umberto Saba!
On *Via San Nicolò* we enter
La Libreria Antica e Moderna,
the bookshop he bought 1914.

Saba's poems let tradition speak
to and though modernity.
He lives today! Yes, he lives
so long as we read his poems.

My journey ends.
And, it is now I "return"
to my armchair and open
my copy of Saba's *Poesie.*

2022 Amici di Guido Gozzano Menzio d'Onore

inspired by Antonio Vivaldi, *Le Quattro Stagioni.*

La Primavera
bird song
friendly chatter
the end of lethargy
prompts me to make a "to do" list –
fresh start

I stir
as do the leaves –
hoe-in-hand, loosen soil
so my garden can breathe again
fresh air

dusk falls
tree frogs echo
the promises we made
to renew our vows and cherish
each day

L'estate
rising
the sun and I
feel ready to tackle
what may come, no matter how hot
the day

voices
children at play
they skitter and scamper
like voles and field mice in meadows
at play

neighbors
chat on the porch
the moon rises, hopes, too …
were the days longer and our dreams
bigger

L'autumno
biscuits
warm, oven-baked
dunked in breakfast black tea
the morning cool, but not chilly
splendid

flannel
and foliage
our favorite fashions
outerwear for people and trees
woven

even
urban dwellers
call it the Harvest Moon
its gilded splendor is mythic
world-wide

L'inverno
somehow
in sleep I hear
the faint falling of snow
under my blanket, like a hare,
burrowed

with care
fear of slipping
I tread the icy path
perhaps in the mail box today
answers

2022 I Colori dell'Anima Best Foreign Poem

Typo-logy

I submitted…
a winter poem about snow peaks,
  but typed peeks;
a spring poem about cherry blossoms,
  but typed cheery;
a summer poem about billowing clouds,
  but typed pillowing;
an autumn poem about fewer gusts,
  but typed guests;
for the Queen's Platinum Jubilee
  from her balcony she pees down upon her people.
Sometimes when what I write is wrong
  it is right.
Some were published!

2022 Ina Coolbrith Circle honorable mention

When Days Get Short

cinquain inspired by Catalan poet Joan Maragall (1860 - 1911)

down beat
growing grim, yet
one day of life is life
how to fight that late autumn dread
Cantar!
2023 California Federation of Chaparral Poets 1st prize

Who ... oops ... Whom Do You Trust?

A Silicon Valley A.I. company
chose me to pose five questions
to test the proficiency
of their prototype CHAT-BOX
designed to simulate conversation.

   Question 1.
If an infinite number of Shakespeares
were left to bang on an infinite number
of typewriters for an infinite number of years,
could they write like a monkey?

   Question 2.
Why is a raven like a writing desk?

   Question 3.
Did the Mad Hatter use a pencil or a pen?

   Question 4.
Did Robert Frost stop by the woods because he was feeling, you
know, kind of religious, or did he take the wrong road and was,
you know, kind of lost?

   Question 5.
Who wrote these questions, me, as in the first person singular
pronoun, or, as in a memory electrode?

2023 California Federation of Chaparral Poets 3rd prize

Poets are the Canis lupus familiaris of Homo sapiens

Both mostly get along on the beach,
but rivals are known to nip.

Dogs will eat almost anything.
Have you seen poets at a conference buffet?

With a little praise
both will eat out of your hand.

Canine ears perk at a dog whistle,
while poets hear words in the wind.

As dogs on a walk sniff the air,
their poet companions can smell spring.

Both howl at the moon,
dogs descendants of wolves; poets, jackals.

Wislawa Szymborska noted that the self-critical jackal
does not exist; I'd say poets are still evolving.

Days draw in, both settle by a fire;
passing gas is to be expected.

Ticks are a source of irritation.
Poets in recital cannot stop yapping.

Incisors bite, canines tear and shred,
molars shear and crush ... editors, of course.

2023 California Federation of Chaparral Poets 3rd prize

Lofty Aspirations

(dedicated to Roy G. Biv)

crevice of dawn
Julia Pfeiffer Burns State Park
from the parking lot
a tunnel under Highway 1
takes you to McWay Falls

gulls outnumbered
by photographers
picturesque a cliché
as the 80 foot cascade
spills onto the beach

in the spraybow
a fusion of colors
this aerial magic
appears and disappears
not an easy shot

under a comforter
back in my Big Sur cabin
dreams
of baby goblins
born behind McWay Falls

*2023 California Federation of Chaparral Poets
honorable mention*

Bio

Neal Whitman lives in Pacific Grove, California, with his wife, Elaine. On the portico to their cottage home is a granite slate incised with a motto in Latin avowed by Henry David Thoreau: *ex lux Oriente, ex fructus Occidente*. Indeed, Neal and Elaine grew up in the East Coast and in retirement as professional educators their lives have come to fruition on the West Coast, specifically on the Monterey Peninsula where the ocean and land inspires their creative impulses. Neal, along with Elaine, is a member of the Yuki Teikei Haiku Society where Neal is a designated dojin. Neal and Elaine were co-editors of the 2021 and 2022 YTHS members anthologies and they co-judge the annual United Haiku and Tanka Society Samurai Haibun contest sponsored by an'ya. Neal also has co-judged the Haiku Society of America annual Merit Book Award and the Tanka Society of America annual Samuel Goldstein Tanka Contest. Neal is the haiku feature editor of *Pulse: Voices from the Heart of Medicine* and is a member of the California Federation of Chaparral Poets and the Ina Coolbrith Circle.

Neal and Elaine are members of *Immagine & Poesia*, an international movement of poets, artists, and musicians founded in Turin, Italy, in 2007, by daughter of Dylan Thomas, Aeronwy Thomas, and, with her passing, is now led by one of its founding members, cara Lidia Chiarelli. Members from over sixty countries profess belief that all art forms are the food for the spirit of new generations.

In what is proudly proclaimed as "America's Last Home Town" Neal has served on the Pacific Grove Advisory Library Board, liaison to the Friends of the Pacific Grove Friends of the Library and also as a member of the Pacific Grove Cultural Arts Commission. He also has volunteered as a docent at the Robinson Jeffers Tor House in Carmel and the Point Pinos Lighhouse in Pacific Grove, as well as providing for the Hospice of the Central Coast one-to- one grief counseling for those who have lost a loved one. Neal's customized auto plate is PG POET set in a frame with the words Chapter and Verse.